# How to.. Festive Winter Floral Designs
## Contempora...
## Flower...

First Published in Britain 2015
Author: Gill McGregor
Designs by: Gill McGregor
Copyright © Gill McGregor  2015
Published by: Gill McGregor College Publishers
ISBN 978-0-9929332-2-7
Printed in the UK
Layout design: www.sosbusyweb.co.uk

Glittered, Waxed Fresh Roses

Gill McGregor

**Coming Soon**

**My Little Black Book of the Elements & Principles For Floral Design**

This 'How to..' make Winter and Festive Designs Book has been created to satisfy the many requests I have received from Flower Arrangers who asked me to write a book on how to make Festive arrangements. The designs incorporated are a range of both Contemporary and Traditional ideas with a host of pictures and narrative to explain their construction. I love the winter season and flowers in the home just lift those cold, dark days.
I hope you enjoy this book as much as I have making it.

*For*
*Contemporary & Traditional Floral Design*

Other Books available from my website www.gillmcgregor.com/books
- Booklet 1 '5 days in a Hotel Bedroom' - a 'How to make' booklet focusing on Autumn and Winter designs
- Booklet 2 'Winning Thruppence shaped my career' – a 'How to make' booklet focusing on Spring and Summer designs
- '50 Techniques Used in Contemporary Floral Designs'
- 'How to.. Contemporary Floral Design - Wire Manipulation'

## To make the radial structure.

Cut 4 straight, dried Cornus alba stems to a length of 80cms. Cut a fifth stem to measure 90cm to form the central straight stem. Thread black beads onto a 1.80mm x 50cm wire secured at each end by hot gluing the last bead at either end of the wire. Repeat using a 1.80mm wire cut to 45cms in length.

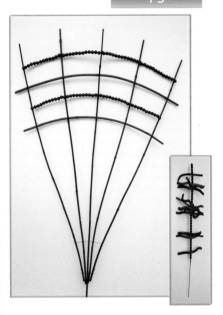

Arrange the Cornus stems to create a radial shape with the longer stem central (which helps insertion) and wire together 3cm from the base of the shorter stems. Secure again 10cms further up by using a metre length of wire bent in half and place around one of the outside stems and twist the wires tightly together until you reach the next stem; place the wires around it and repeat the twisting method until all are secure. Bend the longest beaded wire around a cylindrical waste paper basket to create a curve and secure 5cm down from the top of the Cornus with wire. Repeat the process with the shorter

beaded wire 12.5cms down from the top of the radial Cornus structure.

Cut two 50cm lengths of Cornus and manipulate to a curved shape and weave through the vertical stems to alternate between the beaded wires, secure with wire.

To add a different dynamic I have threaded beads and curved drilled stems onto 1.80mm wires, secured with hot glue at the top and bottom, with sufficient wire left to insert into the floral foam. The structures are now ready to be arranged.

Prepare your floral foam
to extend 5cms (2 inches)
above the rim.

Insert the radial
structure 3cms from the
back of the foam.
Arrange 2 Fatsia japonica
leaves at the front to
hide the vase's rim and
bend the wires of the
threaded structures so
they too can be inserted
for effect.

Further arrange
Fatsias to start to
hide the mechanics.
Add Ilex verticillata
and pine to create
the outline shape and
profile, allowing the
structures to
be seen.

Add a group of red Carnations before arranging 7 Roses to form a vertical zig zag line with a focal point.

Complete the design by hiding the mechanics with small placements of pine.

Use a garland of threaded contorted twigs coiled to fit on a flat

ceramic dish, which can hold water, to act as the mechanics to support foliage and flowers.

3 Red Roses, Pine and Ilex verticillata are arranged amongst the contorted structures, raised at the back for effect. An easy design to construct which complements the radial free standing arrangement.

# Waxed Rose Tubed Design

Prepare your waxed Roses and coned Aspidistra, *see page 54* & construct 5 tubed Aspidistra *see page 20.* Place half a block of soaked floral foam in a flat dish and secure with pot tape. Arrange 5 different height tubed Aspidistra at the back to one side and place your Fatsia leaves at the base of the design to establish the outline and hide the mechanics. Arrange 3 coned Aspidistra as a group at the left base of the tubes for visual balance and start to hide the remaining floral foam with groups of textured foliage. Add baubles on sticks in each of the Aspidistra tubes with a small bauble cluster at the right base of the Aspidistra leaves. Finish with a line of waxed Roses to the left of the tubes and place an additional waxed Rose in each of the Aspidistra cones for effect. Add 2 internally wired bent Equisetum stems (as shown) to evidence the shadowing technique.

This design can be made using different types of bark glued around a new or used posy pad. The secret is to use bark which does not look like it has been cut at the top, so it has a more rustic, natural look. Obviously the base of the bark has to be level so as to be able to sit flat on a charger plate or flat dish.

Select a 20cm posy pad with a 'hard biscuit' base. Rip the bark into lengths to create different sized pieces which can then be individually hot glued into position.

You will find the heat of the glue makes the bark unbearable to touch whilst it sets so use a non conductive implement to push the bark against the posy pad. Once a piece of bark is securely glued, cut the bark level with the posy pad base and repeat until you have covered the entire posy pad's circumference.

# Circular Bark Container Table Arrangement

Arrange the design. Place a wired 'Flameless' LED candle off centre in the foam to provide the height.

Add groups of different flowers and foliage around the candle working outwards towards the bark container at varying height levels. Greater concentration of textures and forms assist the design of this arrangement. Three lengths of Ivy trails were arranged to accentuate space and provide random caging.

A few slithers of bark were positioned in the arrangement to create unity.

This design cannot sit without some form of protection on a surface as it is not water retaining in its design.

The final design was placed on a charger plate to catch excess water leaking from the structure.

This table design is suitable for a coffee table as the star structure is purposefully positioned to be up at the back and down at the front so as not to look flat.

Cut 5 straight dried Cornus alba stems to a length of 45cms. Using 2 stems cross together and secure 3 cms from the top with wire. Repeat the process thus creating a 5 pointed star of even construction.

Using three 0.71mm x 30cm green lacquered stub wires secure to the inner hexagon at three points to provide a means of inserting the structure into the floral foam.

Select a round dish of around 18-20 cms (8 inches) in diameter and fill with a bevelled, half a brick of wet floral foam. Secure with pot tape. Position the Cornus star structure securely with the wires so it is faced rather than flat and with an obvious gap between the structure and the top surface of the floral foam.

Commence by arranging 5 Blue Pine tips into the sides of the wet floral foam under the Cornus star to emphasise the outline shape.

Arrange low groups of flowers, berries and foliage allowing the majority of the star structure to be seen. Vary their height slightly for greater effect. Complete with baubles.

Make the Cornus star as described for the Cornus Star shaped table arrangement.

Decorate each star point with swirls of red Aluminium wire secured with metallic wire.
Cut 3 x 45 cms dried, straight Cornus stems and secure to the inner hexagon at three points to provide a means of holding the star frame.

**To make the hand tied**

Arrange 3 Amaryllis flowers in the centre of the structure, stems parallel and secure with a cable tie making sure you do not damage the hollow stems of the amaryllis.

Place in a suitable vase.

Select a shallow dish which will house a 20cm posy pad with a 'hard biscuit.' Cover the outer edge of the posy pad by pinning artificial snow or white packing material for effect.

Place the disguised posy pad in the dish and arrange bleached Mitsumata branches upside down in the foam.

Add a few tastefully arranged Roses amongst the Mitsumata branches and hide the floral foam with aggregate, wax chippings or decorative sand for textural contrast.

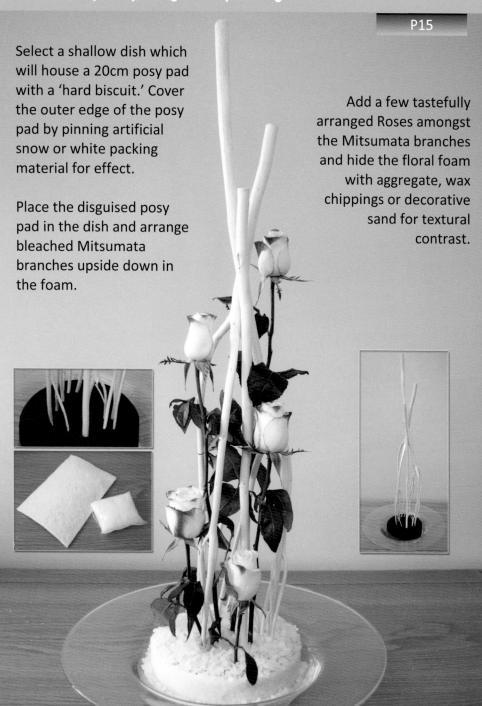

# Hanging Door Spray Hand Tied

Prepare the materials by measuring and cutting Blue Pine so when the Pine sprays are laid on a table they form a triangular shape.

So right handers would do the opposite.

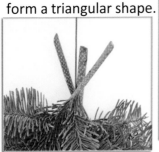

Make sure the stems are clear of needles below where you have decided the binding point will be. During construction the stems are to spiral. As I am a left hander, I place my left materials to go underneath the central, vertical stems and the right stems to lie over the central vertical stems.

# Hanging Door Spray Hand Tied

Arrange the Blue Pine to form a triangular shape with stems spiralling. Arrange one berried pick centrally for effect. Place a second berried pick with additional blue pine fronds to hide the stems.

Add 4 wired fir cones centrally to create a graduated focal line and then securely tie the materials together where you have decided the binding point will be. The binding point must stay in one place for neatness. To disguise the binding point, add and secure a wired ribbon tail and a further large cone before adding a length of plaited string as a means of hanging. Make 2 separate loops of ribbon, each of which are scrunched to Create 'bow' loops and wire to stay in position. To finish the design add the bow loops of

ribbon by pushing the wires through the bound string and position as desired. Once you have checked the positioning of the materials, make sure any wires below the binding point are pushed up into the pine design so they do not protrude and cause potential injury.

Always consider Health and Safety.

P18

Using a decorative tray place an Oasis® foam frames® 25cm ring to sit in its well. Bevel the edges of the foam and wet by pouring ¾ of a pint of water over the ring. To edge the ring, insert short pieces of Blue Pine at a diagonal angle above the 'hard biscuit' so the tips touch the tray and provide a neat round outline.

Repeat and insert very small pieces of Blue Pine to disguise the inner ring's hard biscuit mechanics.

To ensure visually even placement of the focal Brassicas, insert 5 sticks equidistant apart on the upper surface of the foam. Loosely cover the remaining floral foam with Cupressus inserted at an acute diagonal angle before replacing each marker stick with a Brassica.

Using 5 Aspidistra elatior 'Milky Way', arrange so each stem is inserted near a Brassica and manipulate the leaf by twisting and pin to secure with a 0.56mm green lacquered hairpin to fill the central space between the adjacent Brassica.

Arrange concentric patterns of mini Roses, green berried Ivy, and spray

Chrysanthemums to complete the foliage and floral placements.

Five Lily grass blades were arranged to loop around the posy ring to add enclosed space to the design.

Finish by placing a 'Flameless' LED candle into the centre of the design; protect by inserting its base into a clear plastic bag.

Do not use an ordinary wax candle as it would cause a fire hazard if lit.

I love using flat copper rings - they are cheap and easy to find. I am not sure why I thought to try this but I wondered if fir cones could be 'screwed' into a copper ring.
So of course I had to try ; and lo and behold they can.

Using a 30cm (12 inch) flat copper ring, tape with brown florist tape to tone down the colour and to add a bit of physical texture. Tape 2 individual 1.8mm x 50cm stub wires and then tape to the ring on opposite sides to act as insertion legs.

Select the same sized fir cones and insert, one at a time, into the ring and twist until the base of the cone is near the back of the ring, making sure the entire cone is firmly lodged and slide to one of the inner struts. Repeat the process making sure the cones are firmly secure whilst locking together and hiding the inner struts.
Within minutes you have a circular fir cone ring.

Bend each end of the 1.8mm wire legs to form a small loop and then insert the legs towards the outside edges of the wet floral foam in a tall vase. Position the cone ring to be up at the back and down at the front.

To complete the design, add three Fatsia japonica leaves at the base of the wet floral foam to hide the gap between the container and the floral foam.

Measure the height required and using Dracaena 'Green Tie', cut to size, manipulate the leaves to form tubes, pin each with a pearl headed pin and arrange inside the cone ring at the back to provide the tallest placements. Add a line of Roses, remembering to create profile. Add groups of different textured foliage for distinction. Add 2 x three groups of gold baubles and insert a bauble on a stick down each Dracaena tube for effect.

P22

Place half a bevelled brick of wet floral foam on a 20cms (8 inches) diameter flat dish and secure with pot tape.

Using a 25cm flat copper ring tape with brown florist tape to tone down the colour and to add a bit of physical texture. Tape 2 x 1.8mm stub wires 30cms in length and then tape to the ring on opposite sides to act as insertion legs.

Screw the same sized fir cones into the 25cm wreath as previously described on page 20.

Using five cut down Dracaena leaves arrange at the back of the design so they provide part of a circular outline shape; making sure they slightly overlap.

To complete the round outline shape arrange three medium Fatsia japonica leaves.

Take the fir cone ring and bend the ends of the 1.80mm wires to form loops and insert into the wet floral foam within the leaf outline, making sure the ring is up at the back and down at the front for effect.

Cut down two Dracaena leaves and make into tubes; each pinned with a pearl headed pin and arrange between the back of the cone ring and circular outline shape of leaves.

Arrange 3 Roses inside the ring to one side as a group and then complete the design with groups of different textured materials and fir cones.

As this design was made to complement the vertical arrangement with the fir cone ring I have ensured that the same materials have been used for unity.

Using half a block of wet floral foam, cut 2cms (¾ inch) off the bottom and place in a flat dish. To provide the required length, cut 2 x 80cm Draceana leaves straight across and cut up into the leaf, either side of the midrib vein for 10cms (3 inches). Insert the stems into the 2 cm high square of floral foam, making sure the leaf blades lay flat on the top. Place the remainder of the wet foam block on top and secure to the base foam with cut down kebab sticks. Add the Fatsia leaves to complete the outline shape.

Insert the completed fir cone ring structure using the same method previously described so again it faces up at the back and down at the front.

Make 5 different lengths of Dracaena tubes again as previously described and arrange to strengthen the overall length.

This time I have inserted peppers in each for contrasting effect.

Finally arrange 3 Roses inside the ring to one side as a group and then complete the design with groups of different textured materials and fir cones.

As this design was made to complement the vertical arrangement with the fir cone ring I have ensured that the same materials have been used for unity.

**P24**

The starkness of the bleached Mitsumata branches helps provide a more Contemporary winter arrangement.

Select and fill a tall vase with used floral foam before preparing your new, soaked and bevelled floral foam to fit tightly in the vase and extend 5cms (2 inches) above the rim.

Cut the Mitsumata branches to size. I prefer the sides to be asymmetrical, one side longer than the other, for effect. Pin the branches securely to the top surface of the floral foam with a few 0.90mm green lacquered stub wires.

Add a few Fatsia japonica leaves to start to hide the gap between the floral foam and the container and to start to establish the outline shape. Add two Aspidistra elatior 'Variegata' under the Mitsumata branches to strengthen the horizontal line.

Leaf manipulate 4 Aspidistra leaves to create rolled leaves at the tip. Prepare by cutting 0.56mm green lacquered stub wires to a length of 6 cms and bend to form a hair pin shape.

Take one Aspidistra leaf and roll the tip face upwards as desired, making sure the midrib vein stays in line and the hollow is at least 2 fingers in width. Hold in place and insert the wire hairpin on the underside of the leaf, either side of the main vein and fold the wires to cross (like arms folded) to hold the rolled leaf into position.

Arrange the rolled tipped Aspidistra leaves to form a diagonal, horizontal line across the design.

To finish, arrange a horizontal line of Calla Lilies with curved stems. To create their curved stems, after conditioning, remove from the water for 2 hours so the stems start to soften; which helps the manipulation process. Hold the Calla lily in one hand and with the other hand support with a thumb under the stem and fingers diagonally on top of the stem and stroke to create a curve. Arrange the Calla lilies for effect and complete with grouped placements of pine, fir cones and baubles to hide the mechanics and to provide greater textural contrast.

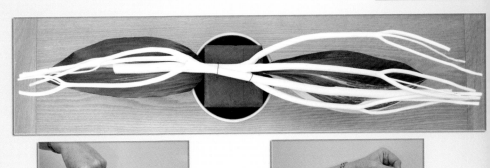

P26

This table design is one of the most extravagant designs in the book, when you consider the number of flower heads that are used, but it's a great talking point and a bit of fun. You will need to slice off the bottom of a 16cm wet foam sphere and stand it on a flat dish.

Each leaf is inserted so the edge of the leaf buffs up against the previous leaf's main vein for neatness.

For this design 30 red Carnations and 15 white Carnations are required.

To make each Carnation go further the calyx is slightly ripped to allow the petals to spread out further. The stems are cut to circa 3cm (1 inch) in length, with leaves removed and the sphere is based working in concentric rings from the base upwards to form a neat, uniform spherical pudding. Towards the top the 'cream' is created using the white Carnations to give the illusion they are pouring down the sides.

To edge the base of the sphere arrange a frill of Common Laurel which will provide a complementary colour scheme and textural contrast. The Laurel leaves are both graduated in size from large at the back to smaller at the front and arranged to be up at the back and lower at the front for effect.

To complete the top is the proverbial Holly with a few Ilex verticillata berries.

1 - Use a 30cm (12 inch) flat wreath ring, secure mossing twine to the inner ring and take 2 handfuls of teased moss; unwanted items, insects and creatures removed.

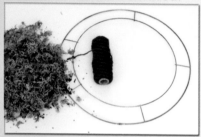

2 - Roll the teased moss into a firm 'sausage' shape.

3 - Place the 'sausage' shaped moss on to the ring. Lift the ring up to bring the mossing twine from underneath the ring towards you.

4 - Wind the twine over the moss towards the void & lift up the ring to bring the twine towards you from underneath. Tug to secure.
Repeat every 3cms. (1 inch)

5 - Take 2 more teased handfuls of moss & roll to create a firm sausage shape and push up against the previous sausage and bind securely to the ring.

6 - Continue to make additional firm moss sausages & bind onto the wreath ring securely.

**7** - Repeat, making sure the moss sausages are firm, not too thick and cover the ring.

**8** - Finish by making a moss sausage the size to fit firmly between the bound sausages to complete a solid moss ring and secure by binding.

**9** - To 'cast off', make a loop with the twine and then lead the ball of twine through the loop and pull to make a knot. Cut the twine and insert the end through a bound twine placement.

**10** - Trim the moss to make a neat and even mossed ring.

Your foundation is now complete ready to make your door wreath.

P30

Take 2 large branches of Blue Pine and prepare by cutting down to make 3 different length piles. Cut the larger lengths; around 20 bushy 'hand sized' (18cm/ 7 inches) pieces, approximately 25 '3 pronged' fronds 14cm (5½ inches) and then 30 small tips 6cm (3 inches).

Moss a 30cm (12 inch) flat copper ring and bind a second 20cm (8 inch) flat copper ring onto the upper surface securely with mossing twine so that part of the ring can be seen inside the void of the mossed wreath. Plait 3 lengths of 60cm (24 inches) mossing twine and place the plaited twine around the wreath and tie the ends together to form a 'hanging loop'. Take a small piece of twine and tie the loop as near to the mossed wreath to stop the hanging loop from moving. Screw 6 identical sized fir cones into the 20cm ring - making sure they are secure.

Tie the end of the mossing twine onto a side of the ring (not at the top or bottom). Begin to base (cover) the 30cm mossed ring by placing a 14cm '3 pronged' frond diagonally

against the outer side of the wreath so its tip touches your work bench and the stem end is on the upper surface of the moss and repeat with a 6cm tip - pointing the same way on the inside of the mossed ring and bind securely with the twine. This is called edging. Repeat with further placements once or twice so that the lengths of pine are in close, neat order; to hide the sides of the mossed ring. Each time try and pull the twine through the needles so when bound tightly the twine cannot be seen amongst the pine. Take an 18cm 'hand sized' length and place on the upper surface to hide the remaining top surface moss and bind so you cannot see the twine. Then repeat by edging the outer and inner rings as before until you can see that an 18cm 'hand sized' frond will hide the top surface. Continue this process until you have based the entire ring. The last placements are the hardest to secure as you need to make sure the twine cannot be seen and then cast off with the loop method.

Add 3 wired fir cones to decorate the centre base of the wreath and arrange 6 more cones to complete the decorative cone circular shape. When inserting wires into the moss make sure it does not come through the back of the moss – otherwise the wires will scratch your door. It is better to insert the wires at an acute diagonal angle into the moss and then face (position) your materials upright or as desired.

Finish with decorative bows and additional wired picks of berries for distinction.

Note: This wreath requires a sheltered position as the fir cones close up when wet.

# Threaded Carnation Free Standing Hand Tied

Threaded Carnations create a fantastic frame to support light weight materials or act as a frill to enhance or show off materials arranged within.

The Carnation is so robust that it can withstand the threading technique using aluminium wire. Here are 3 variations using the same 18 threaded Carnations for you to choose from.

Firstly thread 18 Carnations onto some colour coordinated aluminium wire through each calyx, the outer green part of the flower which holds in the petals, by carefully easing them down the wire.

Once completed cut the wire to allow sufficient to twist together thus forming a round ring of threaded Carnations.

Arrange the stems so they spiral which both looks attractive above and below the water level. The Carnations can be level or up at the back and down at the front.

Once you are happy with the position of the flower heads ensure the binding point Is below vase rim level and bind securely with matching aluminium wire to create a uniform band.

**Design 1**

Cut the stems at a 45 degree angle to the required height and place in a vase. You may need to add scrunched cellophane in the vase to help support the hand tied centrally and vertically.

**Design 1:** Fill with baubles, cones and artificial apples for effect.

**Design 2:** Complete as before but having arranged the Carnation stems to spiral; secure temporarily. Then arrange glittered Birch twigs and slim dried Bulrushes, stems parallel and secure so the binding points of both the dried materials and the fresh Carnations are level with each other. Cut the stems of the Birch hand tied to be circa 15cms long, or much shorter than the Carnations.

Undo the temporary binding point of the Carnation ring and insert the Birch hand tied so the binding points will be level and tightly bind the Carnation stems to secure & create a neat, uniform band.

Add water in the vase so that the Birch and Bulrush stem ends are above the water level to prevent them getting wet and rotting. Place the completed hand tied in the vase and support with scrunched cellophane as appropriate.

**Design 3:** Complete, as design number one, but cut the stems below the banded tying point to 6cms in length. Prepare and secure a piece of wet foam on a flat dish and insert the bundle of stems horizontally into the side of the wet foam.

To give the appearance of a hand tied arrange the stem ends in the other side of the foam to look as if the stems are as one. Make sure you insert the stems the right way round so they can absorb water.

Finish with 4 Aspidistra elatior leaves, 2 as bow loops and 2 cut to represent the tails. Hide the mechanics with a small amount of Blue Pine. Finish the bow with a central Carnation and add a few fir cones in the structure for effect.

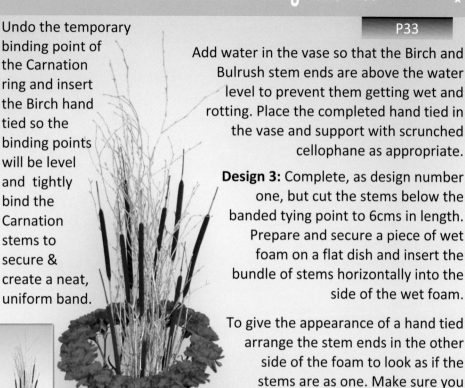

Design 2

Design 3

Large novelties should always be arranged before adding the floral materials. I did use one Fatsia japonica leaf as a 'cushion'.

Adding novelties in a design creates visual impact. The difficulty of incorporating them into an arrangement is how to make sure they don't get damaged whilst making sure they are secure.

I saw this super plush Snowman and had to buy him. For a bit of fun I wanted to place him in a design as a talking point. To protect him from water damage, I used a cut down plastic bag to protect his bottom, secured by a colour coordinated hair toggle.

I used a couple of 0.90mm green lacquered stub wires, bent into hairpins and secured to the 'plastic nappy' with pot tape to assist me in being able to wire him into the design.

The white stick Christmas tree is made from 3 graduated sized triangles bound onto a central stick with metallic wire.

To provide that 'snowy feel' I spray painted with flat white paint; Dracaena leaves, fir cones, pine, Fatsia japonica and Rhapis palm. The outline shape was arranged using the foliage and completed with a line of Avalanche Roses.

I find Equisetum (Snake Grass) one of the most versatile materials to create structures. It is easy to grow, it is easy to source, not expensive and **wow** when internally support wired can be manipulated into so many shapes, containers and structures.

For this coffee table arrangement I have used 2 bunches of Equisetum - the equivalent of 40 stems. Each stem is internally support wired by inserting 50cm x 0.71mm Green Lacquered Stub Wires; both up into the stem and from the tip downwards. Save 2 internally supported stems and use the remaining 38 stems to create the 'plate'.

Once each stem is support wired, take one stem and from the tip start to manipulate the stem into a tight coil. You may find the stem snap at a node don't worry just

carry on until you have the last 10cms of the stem left. If there is a node very near the stem's base, cut it off to allow at least 5cms of hollow stem available. Using a thin black or ordinary steel pin, pin the coil to help keep it in position.

Take a second support wired Equisetum stem and insert the tip into the base of the first stem and then continue to manipulate the stem to increase the size of the coil. You will need to strategically pin the coil into position. You will soon realise when it needs pinning. The pin must be inserted horizontally and you must check each time that the tip of the pin is not sticking out for fear of injury. Each time, cast on by inserting a tip into the hollow of the last Equisetum stem used.

Carry on pinning strategically until you have used all 38 stems or until the desired size. Finish by making sure the last stem is securely pinned. With the remaining 2 internally wired Equisetum stems cut to a

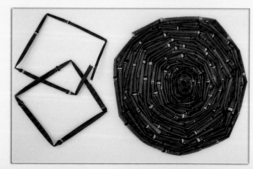

The structure untreated with fresh Equisetum will easily last a week to ten days. I prefer to treat the dish with one part water to one part PVA glue and slop the stirred mixture all over the 'plate' to preserve it so I can re-use it. You will know when the PVA solution is dry as it is white when wet and clear when dry.

length of 52cms. At the end of a stem measure 6cm and bend to form a right angle, measure 12cms and bend to form a right angle, repeat a third and fourth time. With the thinner end, insert into the wired end to form a square. Make another square and then position centrally at the back of the plate and pin diagonally to create a raised plinth for the plate. Check no pins are sticking through the top surface of the plate.

Use a cut down OASIS® green Junior bowl, with the lip removed, fill with floral foam and arrange a few choice flowers and foliage for your desired effect. I have used 3 small Anthuriums 'Tropical', fir for texture and plaited Roebellini.

P38

Your first 2 placements will establish the overall length of the design. Cut a piece of Blue Pine to the required length and then repeat by measuring a second placement so they are identical and insert centrally at each end of the foam brick so the stems touch the top of the tray. Now arrange the stems to create the width using the same method. Arrange additional stems to create the overall outline shape, oval or diamond; all the tips of the foliage point downwards to hide the tray.

Arrange more Blue Pine, inserted at an acute diagonal angle to cover the wet foam, utilising all parts of the foam brick; this is called 'greening up'.

This oval table arrangement with a distinctive Hogarth curve ('Lazy S') placement of connected fir cones demonstrates the text book method of arranging oval or diamond shape designs with obvious lines of movement.

Using an OASIS® green Single Brick Tray cut off 2cms from the side of a brick of wet foam and place centrally in the tray to provide a well either side to act as a watering hole. Secure the brick towards each end with pot tape and pin 0.71mm hair pins either side of the tape to aid security.

Prepare 2 strands of graded interconnected fir cones. Cut a length of Aluminium wire, tightly wind an end around the base of the smallest fir cone making sure the wire is as 'invisible' as possible. Secure the next cone by winding the aluminium wire around its base so the cones are interlocked together and the wire can hardly be seen. Repeat, with graded sized cones to make half the desired overall length and then make the other wired cone length.

Insert centrally a wired 'flameless' LED Candle into the design and pin the interconnecting cone strands on to the top of the blue pine to form a Hogarth Curve ('Lazy S' shape).

Arrange a central line of Roses to provide a raised profile towards the candle. Zig zag the placements either side of an imaginary central line equidistant apart.

Arrange 5 spray Roses each side of the candle again, providing a raised profile to establish the width of the design.

Within each 'quarter', two distinctive lines of like materials are arranged which flow diagonally from one side of the arrangement to the other, each with a raised profile.

The oval table arrangement is completed with a line of individual Ivy leaves and Ivy trails to give form and textural contrast.

Arranging lines allow each selected plant material to be seen to its best advantage and this style of arranging is often used commercially to enable each selected component to be best seen visually. Giving each placement space also helps the visual impact.

lacquered stub wire hair pins to either end of the branch to further aid security.

Insert the wired branch stem to a depth of 10cms into the vase and impale the sphere on the top of the branch. Bind the branch at the base of the sphere with a band of pot tape to prevent the sphere slipping down. Very lightly water the sphere. Do not soak the sphere as if normal floral foam as it will become far too heavy to use.

Actual balance and stability are the most important aspects of making a topiary arrangement. The materials selected to create the topiary should also be long lasting as it is difficult to water the topiary shape.

Select a reasonably heavy ceramic container and weigh it down further with some stones at the bottom before adding tightly packed wet floral foam which eventually extends 4cms beyond the rim of the vase.

Saw a Silver Birch branch to the correct length adding an extra 10cm each end for insertion into the floral foam and into a 16cm wet foam sphere. Tape 0.90mm green

The secret of hiding the topiary's mechanics is to firstly arrange an overall wash of light weighted Cupressus, inserted at an acute diagonal angle to lie against the topiary sphere, pinned down with 0.56mm green lacquered stub wire hairpins where necessary. This will hide the majority of the mechanics before adding identical sized placements of Holly and Ilex verticillata evenly for effect.

Finish by arranging materials in the weighted vase, in lines and groups of textural and form contrast, at the base of the branch; 3 rolled Prunus laurocerasus (Common Laurel) were added for effect.

**Design 2**:  A similar covered 16cm wet sphere placed on a frill of Fatsia japonica leaves in a shallow dish can make a complementary coffee table design.

**Design 3**: The same sphere can be put on 5 equidistant, identical length Cornus legs to raise the design and placed on a shallow dish. To aid distinction 2 identical sized cornus triangles are constructed and placed over the sphere to rest centrally. Pin the 6 sided Cornus star into position with 0.71mm green lacquered stub wire hair pins.

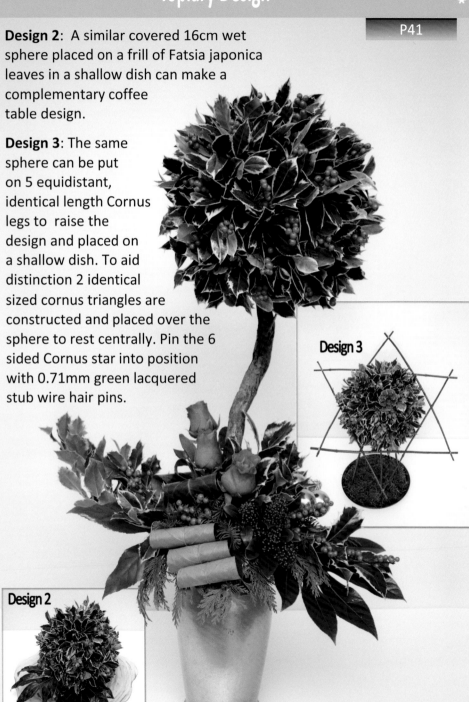

Design 3

Design 2

Make 2 domed white Carnation structures: one with seven Carnations the other

with 14 Carnations.
Remove the leaves of each Carnation so only the top node has leaves remaining.
Select a strong straight stemmed Carnation for the centre and position the Carnations around the central Carnation so their heads form a dome whilst their stems are parallel with each other.
Use a mirror to check they are uniformly domed and when you are happy with their position bind to secure with decorative aluminium wire to form a tight, neat, uniform band.

When both structures have been made, prepare your container and arrange 2 Phormium tenax 'Black Beauty' to form a frame by slitting the slightly longer leaf to allow the other leaf tip to be threaded through. The stems are positioned right at the outside edges of the container to ensure there is sufficient room for the mass of Carnation stems.

Arrange both Carnation structures securely into the wet foam with the smaller structure at the top. You can now add your Fatsia japonica leaves to start to hide the mechanics and rim of the vase. Finish by adding groups of berried Ivy, Senecio greyii, and Pine; which have obvious different forms,

textures and colouration.

To add a Christmassy feel, a group of silver baubles and a knotted chain of crystals from a belt purchased from a renown cheap clothes chain complete the design.

I have used this fun design many times as it is easy and cheap to make and can be made at a height suitable for a central table decoration.

Using 1 bunch (20 stems) of Equisetum (Snake Grass) internally support wire 7 large, straight stems of Equisetum by inserting a 50cm x 0.71mm Green Lacquered Stub Wire up each stem. Take one internally support wired stem and place the remaining 6 to go around the central stem 10cms from its base and secure with both a rubber band and finally covered with pot tape to create the 'trunk'. Insert a kebab stick into the central stem to provide additional supporting strength.

Internally support wire from the bottom and the top the remaining 13 Equisetum stems and then place each around the 'trunk' level, make sure they are level and then secure tightly together at your desired 'trunk' height.

Bend each Equisetum stem at right angles just above the pot tape and, with a pre-made measuring stick, measure 15cms before bending each stem upwards.

In turn place the tip of the now triangular Equisetum stem to spiral around the central trunk until a conical shape has been made.

Check placements are both level and evenly spaced and bind the tips to the trunk neatly and securely with colour coordinated metallic wire.

When positioning the trunk in floral foam, mark where you wish it to be inserted and gouge out around one centimetre deep of floral foam with a spoon and then insert the trunk into the hole and push down until secure. If wobbly insert wire hairpins diagonally through the trunk into the foam for extra stability.

Decorate the base of the floral foam as desired.

**Alternatively**

Use the Equisetum Christmas tree as part of a hand tied to 'cage' a few choice flowers and place in a vase to create a talking point.

A traditional design has definite dimensions. The height is one and half times the height of the container. The arms must measure the same length as the height of the container. The central profile at the base of the design should measure half the height of the container.

It is important to appreciate that every floral design is seen side on as well as from the front; we walk around an arrangement so the profile is very, very important.

I prefer to arrange the arms and profile just above the container before adding the height.

So as this is a very traditional design I have arranged a 'wash' of Cupressus first to establish the base outline shape to hide the gap between the floral foam and the container before adding my choice material, Blue Pine, measured as stated above to firmly establish the base outline shape.

Now arrange the height; one and a half times the height of the container. Place the tallest, central stem one finger thickness from the back of the foam and then arrange further stems to create a symmetrical triangular outline shape.

Once happy with the overall outline shape start to hide the mechanics with foliage positioned on the sides and top of the floral foam. Add additional filler material.
I have used Eryngium to provide textural and form contrast which will eventually become the visually recessed material upon final completion.

Having arranged a symmetrical outline shape with profile, the flowers can be added. So to suit the container I elected to use Avalanche Roses as they have a 'vintage' look.

Place the three at the top to provide the point. Then arrange the placements at the base to provide the width and profile. With the remainder create patterns of partly concentric circles with space in between to complete the design with an obvious focal flower at the front from which all materials should appear to radiate from.

With practice you will find it unnecessary to physically measure the materials as your minds eye will be able to let you know the length of cut material required.

Once the Roses are arranged add further foliage and filler material to disguise the mechanics.

 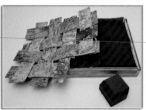 

Silver Birch bark has a wintery feel which oozes textural contrast. It is therefore a must for winter designs to give that frosty feel whilst enhancing plant material.

Select a shallow square container and line with strips of bark before cutting wet floral foam to fill the container to the rim.

Cut lengths of birch bark to size to slightly extend beyond the container on all sides.
I have cut mine to 5cms wide and 28cms in length.

Weave the bark to form a woven 'mat'. The thickness of the bark will prevent you getting the lengths to totally line up against each other. I don't see that there is a problem seeing a very small amount of the dark green foam through the 'mat'. But if you don't like it you could always stick some additional bark underneath with hot glue to hide the gaps. Strategically hot glue the lengths together to secure the 'mat' into position. Cut a square corner of the mat away to allow an additional bevelled, square of wet floral foam to be pinned with kebab sticks into position to provide the mechanics for the arrangement. Cut a small stem of Cymbidium Orchids to your desired length/ height and arrange to establish the focal line. Knot 3 x Phormium tenax 'Black Beauty' and position to form a line down one side.

Add groups of black berried Ivy, flowering Skimmia japonica and silver Eryngium at different height levels, yet lower than the Orchids to hide the mechanics, provide different forms and complete the outline shape. For unity add a few slithers of the Silver Birch Bark in the arrangement.

### Alternatively

Remove the cage of a 7 x 18cm Wet Foam WEDDING BELLE® Bouquet Holder to gain access to the floral foam. Remove the foam and line the half plastic ball with a thick plastic bag and reassemble to prevent water leaking out. Saw the tip end off the handle.

Using an eight inch floral base support, insert the handle to achieve the support required and secure to the spear with pot tape. Wire the woven square previously made to the base support, by threading wire around one of the woven horizontal bands and twisting the wire around the spear to create the Look of a container.

Arrange the foliage to provide the required outline shape. Complete with groups of materials of different forms and textures. Stage the design on a charger plate with a small amount of wet foam at the base holding an arranged selection of complementary materials.

Certain vases do not lend themselves to be filled with floral foam to keep the flowers in position and so a hand tied is a solution.

Regardless of size, the secret of making a successful hand tied is that you have sufficient central materials, visible or not, to act as your mechanics.

These identical vases do not have the means to hold floral foam. I have used 2 Christmas picks and removed the artificial leaves to provide a central mechanic of red artificial berries and wired fir cones for each hand tied.

I have support wired using the stitched method 2 lots of three Ivy leaves. Take a 0.38mm green lacquered stub wire and make a small stitch from the back, one third down from the tip of the Ivy leaf either side of the midrib vein. Bend the wire to form a soft loop, without tearing the leaf and wind the longer wire around the shorter wire and the Ivy stem. This will allow you to manipulate the leaf to curve around the vase.

Select and clean the stems of the mini white Roses and white Eryngium. Hold the berry and cone pick and separate into 3 key groups. Between each group add, with stems spiralling, a single Rose. When all 3 are arranged thread through the berry cone pick 2 Roses to create the central height. Complete with 3 spiralled stems of Eryngium followed by the placement of 3 loops of China grass and finish with a frill of three stitched Ivy leaves. As there are so few materials the stems will not look as though they are spiralling. Check placements before securing into position with a small cable tie. Cut the stems to required length and insert the hand tied into the vase.

Repeat to make a second design and insert into the second vase.

Interconnect the two placements by inserting a blade of China grass into the hand tieds for effect.

Place floral foam to fill a selected container, with the height of the foam 3cms (1 inch) lower than the rim. Insert 8 Cornus alba stems equidistant apart to form a conical shape and bind securely at the top with metallic wire. Add additional, varying lengths of Cornus diagonally to create an interesting, transparent conical shape.

Arrange an outline of Skimmia japonica to curve around one side of the structure. Hide the floral foam inside the Cornus cone with short placements of Skimmia. Add 10 Roses to flow around the structure and finish with berried picks to aid distinction.

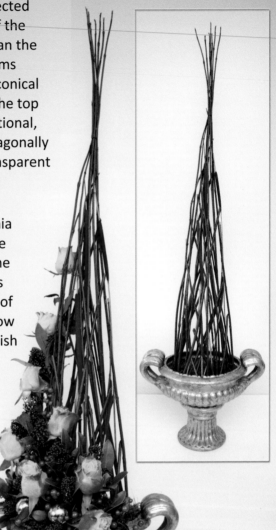